Find
Your
Source

Sara Miller McCune founded SAGE Publishing in 1965 to support the dissemination of usable knowledge and educate a global community. SAGE publishes more than 1000 journals and over 800 new books each year, spanning a wide range of subject areas. Our growing selection of library products includes archives, data, case studies and video. SAGE remains majority owned by our founder and after her lifetime will become owned by a charitable trust that secures the company's continued independence.

Los Angeles | London | New Delhi | Singapore | Washington DC | Melbourne

SUPER
QUICK
SKILLS

Find
Your
Source

Gary
Thomas

Los Angeles | London | New Delhi
Singapore | Washington DC | Melbourne

Los Angeles | London | New Delhi
Singapore | Washington DC | Melbourne

SAGE Publications Ltd
1 Oliver's Yard
55 City Road
London EC1Y 1SP

SAGE Publications Inc.
2455 Teller Road
Thousand Oaks, California 91320

SAGE Publications India Pvt Ltd
B 1/I 1 Mohan Cooperative Industrial Area
Mathura Road
New Delhi 110 044

SAGE Publications Asia-Pacific Pte Ltd
3 Church Street
#10-04 Samsung Hub
Singapore 049483

© Gary Thomas 2019

Images © Gettyimages.com

First published 2019

Apart from any fair dealing for the purposes of research or private study, or criticism or review, as permitted under the Copyright, Designs and Patents Act, 1988, this publication may be reproduced, stored or transmitted in any form, or by any means, only with the prior permission in writing of the publishers, or in the case of reprographic reproduction, in accordance with the terms of licences issued by the Copyright Licensing Agency. Enquiries concerning reproduction outside those terms should be sent to the publishers.

Editor: Jai Seaman
Editorial assistant: Lauren Jacobs
Production editor: Katherine Haw
Proofreader: Clare Weaver
Marketing manager: Catherine Slinn
Cover design: Shaun Mercier
Typeset by: C&M Digitals (P) Ltd, Chennai, India
Printed in the UK

Library of Congress Control Number: 2019935895

British Library Cataloguing in Publication data

A catalogue record for this book is available from the British Library

ISBN 978-1-5264-8883-1

At SAGE we take sustainability seriously. Most of our products are printed in the UK using responsibly sourced papers and boards. When we print overseas we ensure sustainable papers are used as measured by the PREPS grading system. We undertake an annual audit to monitor our sustainability.

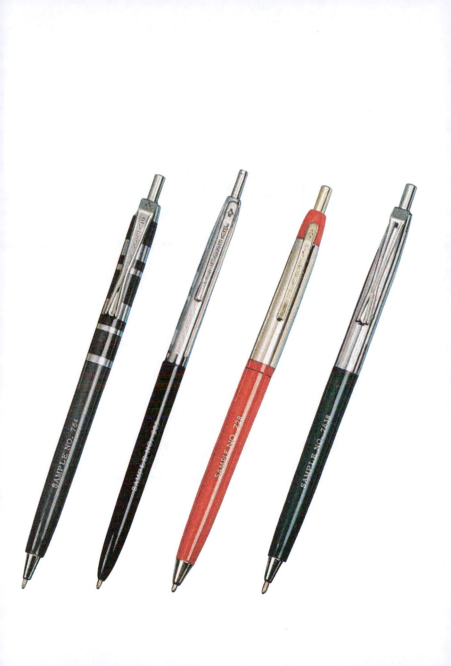

Contents

Everything
in this book!

Section 1   What is a source?

Sources are places or people from which we get information. In this section you will learn about the sources we use in academic life: books, journal articles, reports, and websites.

Section 2   How do I know if it's a good source?

A good source is based in research or scholarship. This section will give you the tools you need to spot a credible source.

Section 3   How are primary and secondary sources different?

Primary sources are straight from the horse's mouth – from the person who has done the research or had the experience. Secondary sources marshal together other people's research, ideas, thoughts, or experiences. This section will explore these differences in more detail.

Section 4   Where do I go online to search?

Good places to start any online search are Google Scholar and Google Books. In section 4 you will learn some tricks for getting the most out of your searches online.

Section 5   What's the point of the library?

You will find a vast array of resources and databases on your library website which will give you access to a much broader array of sources than, say, Google Scholar. This section will explain the importance and usefulness of libraries.

Section 6   What's a database? And why is it good for me?

A database is just a big bag with lots of organized information in it that you can find easily. There are subject databases that carry information on specific subjects, and then there are bigger generic databases that combine other, smaller databases. This section will explain these differences and how to use databases, portals, and platforms to your advantage.

Section 7   Where do I find stuff that's not in the big databases?

For official statistics, theses and images, there's a whole range of sources you may not be aware of, but are really useful to know. Section 7 will give you some tips for how to locate these handy resources.

Section 8   Who will help me?

Well, librarians, obviously. And your tutors. But also try social networking with specialist websites that connect you with others doing academic work. Section 8 will provide you with some great social media sites and platforms that would be beneficial for you to use during your studies.

Section 9   Why can't I find anything?

If you can't find anything (or you find too much) you'll need to broaden your field of vision (or narrow it). To open up your vista, you can draw a mindmap or try 'snowballing', or there are various tricks you can use with databases to focus your search.

What is a source?

10 second summary

Sources are places or people from which we get information. For practical purposes in academic life, they are books, journal articles, reports, and websites.

60 second summary

What is an academic source?

To do academic work of any kind – writing an essay or doing a research project – you need evidence, and there are many **sources** of evidence. For example, the source may be:

- literature – books, journal articles, websites

- personal experience – what you see and hear

- the testimony of others – what other people say

- documents or archives – records of things having happened, statistics of various kinds, diaries

- artefacts – objects which reveal or evoke an activity, idea, place, or time

- observation – systematically watching to see what happens

… or any combination of these.

However, when we talk about **sources** in academic life – whether that's writing a dissertation or completing an assignment – we are usually talking about the first of these, literature: in books, journals, and online sources, and it is finding these sources that I'll concentrate on in this book.

What do you mean by literature?

Literature can be almost anything that represents the results of research or scholarship on a subject. It is written material that may appear in:

- books

- articles

- conference and symposium proceedings

- dissertations and theses

- websites

- research reports

These sources are of different kinds, and they will be viewed differently by your tutors. I'll look at the quality of sources in Section 2.

Article – a write-up of research or scholarship in a **journal**, presenting research findings or discussing topics of interest.

Journal – a periodical which carries **articles** (usually **peer-reviewed**) on topics of interest (usually arising from research) to academics and students of a subject.

Sources is the shorthand for all of these.

Conference – a gathering of academics, professionals, and students meeting to discuss topics in a subject area.

'It's not where you take things from – it's where you take them to.'
Jean-Luc Godard

Test yourself!

Jot down your thoughts in the table below

	✓	Notes
First thoughts: where might your main sources be?		

How do I know if it's a good source?

10 second summary

Make sure it's based in research or scholarship. Make sure it's not just someone's opinion.

60 second
summary

Think for yourself

Some sources have more credibility than others, and you must be careful
not to be taken in by something just because it's in print. When you use
a source, remember that tutors will be looking to see if you can think for
yourself. They'll especially want to see that you seem to be suspicious
of certain kinds of thinking. They'll also want to see that you are wary
of any line of reasoning that comes from a vested interest or a strongly
held opinion.

What makes a source good or bad (or somewhere in-between)?

Has it got 'bottom'? Ask the following questions of it:

- Is it a primary or secondary source? We'll look at this in the next section.

- What is the nature and credibility of the publication it appears in? Is it a **peer-review** journal? Peer-review is the process by which an article is appraised by a group of experts (called 'peers') before it is accepted for publication. Only articles given the green light by the experts are published in a peer-review journal.

- Is this literature written following a piece of research?

- Or, if it is not a piece of research appearing in a journal, is it, by contrast, someone's opinion? Who is the person? What authority do they have? Do they have any vested interests?

Peer-review – a system used by editors of scholarly journals to assess the quality of work submitted for publication. Submissions to a peer-review journal will be assessed by two or more experts in a field, and using these assessments a journal editor will judge whether a submission is worthy of publication. Publication in a peer-review journal is taken to be the most robust assurance of an article's quality.

How to think critically about the source

At university, your tutors will be looking not just for *what* you know – not, in other words, for 'facts' – but for your *attitude* to knowledge. So, they'll be looking to see what kind of sources you are seeking and how you 'read'

Secondary source – is a presentation of, and/or reworking of, usually, many **primary sources**.

those sources. Are you reading them critically, as if they may contain mistakes, omissions or biases, or are you taking everything they offer as the gospel truth?

You can employ critical thinking about sources that you encounter – any piece of research or any scholarly argument – in your literature review by asking yourself these questions:

Sources – sources of evidence such as literature, personal experience, testimony, documents, archives, artefacts. In academic life (and in this book), we are mainly talking about literature of one kind or another.

- Are there any vested interests at play?

- Might the writers' objectives in undertaking the research sway their reasoning in some way?

- Would different methods have yielded different findings?

Literature review – an organized review of books, articles, and published research on a specific topic to discover themes, gaps, inconsistencies, agreements.

- What sources of information are the writers or researchers themselves drawing upon – is there evidence of balance, or are the writers' own sources being 'cherry-picked'?

- What is the quality of the data being drawn upon – is it well-referenced from good primary sources?

- Is the writer's reasoning sound? If you were arguing with them, what would you say?

'... the answers you get from literature depend on the questions you pose.'
Margaret Atwood

Check your understanding

Write in your answers

	✓	Notes
1 Can you distinguish between a peer-review and non-peer-review journal?		
2 What might you do to spot contract research?		
3 How would you assess if authors have vested interests?		

How are primary and secondary sources different?

10 second summary

Primary sources are straight from the horse's mouth – from the person who has done the research or had the experience. Secondary sources marshal together other people's research, ideas, or experiences.

60 second summary

What are primary and secondary sources?

- A primary source is a direct account of what has been done or observed from the individual who completed the research, or had the experience.

- A secondary source is a reworking of, usually, many primary sources. Textbooks are the most common form of secondary source.

In practice, it's difficult sometimes to distinguish between a primary and a secondary source, so you shouldn't get too worried about strict boundaries between them. And there is no automatic correlation between the quality of a source and its 'primary-ness' or 'secondary-ness'. Some primary sources may be very suspect (because, for example, they are about flimsy research), while some secondary sources may be excellent.

Examples of primary sources

- reports of original research or scholarship in a journal

- autobiographies

- government documents and statistics

- correspondence (including electronic kinds, such as email)

- original documents (such as birth certificates) or artefacts

- photographs and audio or video recordings

- speeches

- technical reports

Examples of secondary sources

- textbooks

- biographies

- dictionaries and encyclopaedias

- review articles

Collaboration

A relatively new and increasingly important source is the **collaboration** that brings together high-quality sources and then synthesizes and summarizes the findings for the reader. One of these, for medics and others in healthcare, is the Cochrane Collaboration (www.cochrane.org/ or for Twitter see @cochranecollab).

Follow the flowcharts on the next pages to see the advantages and disadvantages of primary and secondary research.

Primary sources – why they're good, or not so good

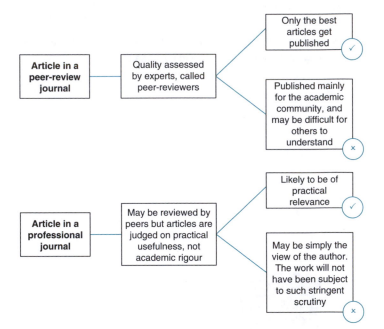

Article in a peer-review journal → Quality assessed by experts, called peer-reviewers

- Only the best articles get published ✓
- Published mainly for the academic community, and may be difficult for others to understand ✗

Article in a professional journal → May be reviewed by peers but articles are judged on practical usefulness, not academic rigour

- Likely to be of practical relevance ✓
- May be simply the view of the author. The work will not have been subject to such stringent scrutiny ✗

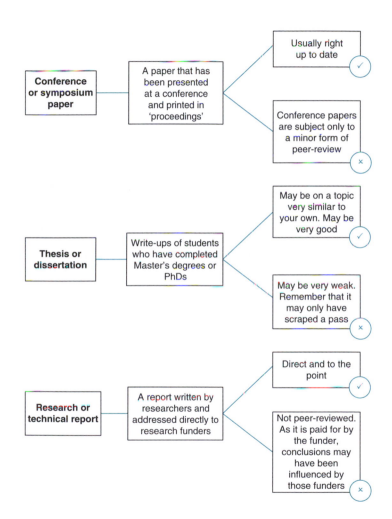

Conference or symposium paper — A paper that has been presented at a conference and printed in 'proceedings'

- Usually right up to date ✓
- Conference papers are subject only to a minor form of peer-review ✗

Thesis or dissertation — Write-ups of students who have completed Master's degrees or PhDs

- May be on a topic very similar to your own. May be very good ✓
- May be very weak. Remember that it may only have scraped a pass ✗

Research or technical report — A report written by researchers and addressed directly to research funders

- Direct and to the point ✓
- Not peer-reviewed. As it is paid for by the funder, conclusions may have been influenced by those funders ✗

Secondary sources – why they're good, or not so good

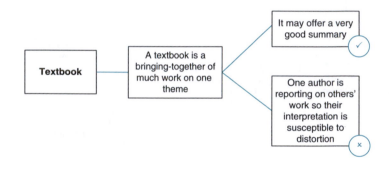

Textbook

A textbook is a bringing-together of much work on one theme

It may offer a very good summary ✓

One author is reporting on others' work so their interpretation is susceptible to distortion ✗

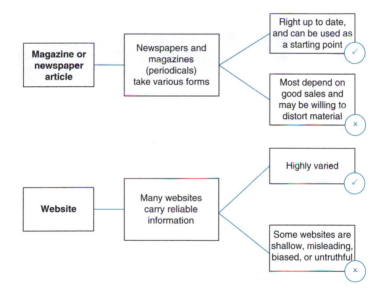

A note about Wikipedia

Wikipedia is a secondary source and is usually excellent. However, because it can be edited by anyone it may be misleading, particularly about controversial topics, or people. Certain political figures, for example, may be subjected to organized campaigns of disinformation.

A student told us

'I'm not sure if I can use Wikipedia as a source.'

It's best not to use direct quotes from it, but click the links to the references (bottom of the Wikipedia page) from which the Wikipedia entry is built.

No good or bad

You can probably see from the flowcharts that the simple equations of ...

Primary source = Good, and

Secondary source = Bad
... are misleading.

Primary sources are usually good, but when it comes to published literature sources, being primary doesn't automatically guarantee quality. And some textbooks – secondary sources – are excellent. The thing to do is to evaluate them on their own terms.

Primary source – a direct account of what has been done or observed. Compare with **secondary source.**

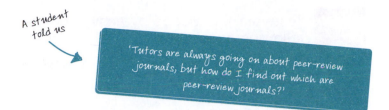

A student told us

'Tutors are always going on about peer-review journals, but how do I find out which are peer-review journals?'

The best peer-review journals are listed in the Web of Science. Search for 'Web of Science list of journals', which you can access through your library website. Ask a librarian for help if necessary.

Things to remember

- Use primary sources if you can, or at least show that you have gone beyond looking at textbooks by referencing some key primary sources.

- Try to avoid using only one source; wherever possible corroborate and verify from others.

- By reading from a variety of sources you will get a more rounded picture of the topic.

'"Classic" – a book which people praise and don't read.'

Mark Twain

CHECK POINT

Test your knowledge by answering the following questions

	✓	Notes
1 Can you distinguish between a primary and a secondary source?		
2 What might be the relative benefits of primary and secondary sources?		

Congratulations

You've thought about the quality of various sources

Now … how to find them.

Where do I go online to search?

10 second summary

Good places to start any online search are Google Scholar and Google Books. They point you in the right direction and may find you a key source from which you can 'snowball'.

60 second summary

Google Scholar is your best friend!

Google Scholar is a great starting point when searching for information online. It works in much the same way as Google, but it is more targeted at the kinds of source material you will be looking for in university life. Just search for 'Scholar' from the main search box to get started.

You use Google Scholar in the same way that you would have used Google. That is to say, you can type in a question or a more targeted inquiry based on a particular article that you have already identified.

Using Google Scholar

Imagine that you're a psychology student interested in what Bowlby's attachment theory might offer for an understanding of stalking.

Overleaf are the 'answers' I got when I typed the words **attachment theory stalking** into Google Scholar. The figure shows the various elements of the Scholar 'answer' page.

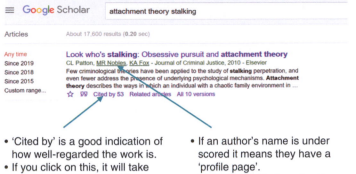

≡ **Google** Scholar   attachment theory stalking

Articles   About 17,600 results (0.20 sec)

Any time
Since 2019
Since 2018
Since 2015
Custom range...

Look who's stalking: Obsessive pursuit and attachment theory
CL Patton, MR Nobles, KA Fox - Journal of Criminal Justice, 2010 - Elsevier
Few criminological theories have been applied to the study of **stalking** perpetration, and
even fewer address the presence of underlying psychological mechanisms. **Attachment
theory** describes the ways in which an individual with a chaotic family environment in ...
☆ 99 Cited by 53 Related articles All 10 versions

- 'Cited by' is a good indication of how well-regarded the work is.
- If you click on this, it will take you to all the works that have cited this work.

- If an author's name is under scored it means they have a 'profile page'.
- Click on this: their work will probably be close to the subject you're researching.

Google and the Google logo are registered trademarks of Google LLC, used with permission.

There are other ways of using Google Scholar to find sources

You can:

- Type into the search box the full reference for an article. Scholar will emerge with the full details of the article and the abstract.

- Type a key author's name into the search box and Scholar will emerge with everything that they've written. This is easier if the author's name is Xavier Sweedlepipe than if it's Joan Smith. If you are unlucky enough to have an urgent need for Joan Smith, you can try adding a phrase relevant to your inquiry, such as 'Joan Smith economic recovery'. This will focus your search.

- Download the Google Scholar Button. Once you've downloaded this app (which you can usually do from Google Scholar itself), the blue 'button' will sit in your Chrome toolbar and you can then click on this in any webpage for easy access to any article. For example, if I type in 'anthrax toxin protective antigen' into the Button's search box I get the results shown below.

Finding and using the Google Scholar Button from Chrome browser

• Google Scholar button

• 'Related articles' takes you to a raft of connected articles. Really useful: try it.

• This is where you can download the article.

Google and the Google logo are registered trademarks of Google LLC, used with permission.

Google Scholar features

One particularly useful feature of Google Scholar is that it will give you alternative referencing formats for a particular article. So, if I type in the name of an article to the Google Scholar search box, for example:

Shaw, A. and Shea, S. (2006) The more you read, the more you know. Paediatric Child Health, 11(9): 566.

… the Google answer page will emerge with the article and a little 🔖 sign at the bottom of the page, which lets you choose amongst various referencing formats for the article, like this …

Cite	
MLA	Shaw, Alyson, and Sarah Shea. "The more you read, the more you know." (2006): 566-566.
APA	Shaw, A., & Shea, S. (2006). The more you read, the more you know.
Chicago	Shaw, Alyson, and Sarah Shea. "The more you read, the more you know." (2006): 566-566.
Harvard	Shaw, A. and Shea, S., 2006. The more you read, the more you know.
Vancouver	Shaw A, Shea S. The more you read, the more you know.

BibTeX   EndNote   RefMan   RefWorks

And you'll note also that at the bottom of the page you can choose to insert the reference into one of several reference managers.

Your tutors will have told you which referencing format preferred at your university. If they haven't, ask them.

Google and the Google logo are registered trademarks of Google LLC, used with permission.

Librarians will point out that Google Scholar won't necessarily take you to the best sources. Also, be aware that focusing is particularly difficult, given that Scholar searches cover 'All fields' and Boolean searches aren't possible. However, it's a great place to start, and you can then supplement it with targeted databases if you need them.

Google Books

There is also Google Books, which will find relevant books, point you to the page(s) relevant to your search inquiry, and even show you the page(s) themselves. From the Google main homepage, just type 'Google books' directly into the search box.

Other search engines are available

… of course. You can try Microsoft Academic Search, and others that you can find at EasyBib.

Snowballing

If you are lucky enough to find a source from Google Scholar (or another search engine) that looks just right – or at least as close as you think you're going to get to perfection – try **snowballing** from it. This means using your key reference to lead you forwards in time to sources that have cited it, or backwards to sources upon which the authors themselves drew. From this key reference you can:

- Borrow its keywords for further searches

- Use its reference list to identify additional papers (called 'backward snowballing')

Paper – an **article**, but 'paper' usually refers to a presentation (which may be written up later for **proceedings**) given at a **conference** or **symposium**.

- Look at the papers that have cited it to see if there are relevant or linked sources (called 'forward snowballing')

- See which journals are carrying papers on the topic you're interested in

Symposium – like a **conference,** but on a more specific topic within the subject area. Papers given at symposia are often published in **proceedings**.

ACTIVITY Test your snowballing skills!

Imagine that you are a computer sciences student interested in online security, and your tutor has referred you to a symposium paper which she can't remember the title of exactly, but it's by a group of people, of whom she remembers that Tom Chothia was one, and it had 'anonymity' in the title. So, you type 'Tom Chothia anonymity' into the Google Scholar search box. Scholar comes up immediately with the answer:

Arapinis, M., Chothia, T., Ritter, E. and Ryan, M., 2010, July. Analysing unlinkability and anonymity using the applied pi calculus. In Computer Security Foundations Symposium (CSF), 2010 23rd IEEE (pp. 107–121). IEEE.

(No, the title means absolutely nothing to me, either, but you can still snowball. Promise.)

Now:

1 Find this article on Google Scholar. (Try using just the three words I used: Tom;Chothia;anonymity.)

2 Backward snowball by accessing a publicly available version of the paper (right-hand side of the Google Scholar screen) and looking at its reference list. Which references look best? You could try Googling interesting-looking ones to see which have been heavily cited.

A student told us

'I panic if I lose the details of a quotation.'

3   Forward snowball by clicking at the bottom of the Google Scholar answer entry by clicking on the link that says Cited by 132. You now have all 132 of the articles that have cited the Chothia paper since it was published. Are there any that have been particularly heavily cited, or which are interesting because they are both heavily cited and recent?

4   Do the same – backward and forward snowballing – with an article from your own subject area.

'Always read something that will make you look good if you die in the middle of it.'

P.J. O'Rourke

Type a sentence from the quotation into the Google main homepage in double quotation marks: "bla bla bla". (The double quotation marks tell Google to find only and exactly only this phrase.) Google may, if you're lucky, actually find the page in the book and refer you on to Google Books, where you'll be able to get the details you want.

Jot down your answers in the table below

	✓	Notes
1 Have you tried typing in a general inquiry to Google Scholar?		
2 Have you downloaded the 'Google Button'?		
3 Type in the details of a specific article to Google Scholar: author, title, and journal name.		

Congratulations

You've used an all-purpose search engine, in Google Scholar.

Now … broaden out your search using your library's resources.

What's the point of the library?

10 second
summary

You will find a vast array of resources and databases on your library website which will give you access to a much broader range of sources than, say, Google Scholar. You'll also be able to focus your search better using the online tools that the library provides.

60 second summary

Make the most of your library

Most, if not all, university libraries enable you to access, without paying, a huge range of books, journals, and other resources via a central jumping-off point. That jumping-off point at my university, the University of Birmingham, is called FindIt@Bham. The one at yours will be called something similar, such as iDiscover or SOLO or Library Search. These will provide the perfect basis for you to find great sources of information to inform your research.

Ask a librarian!

You'll be offered a guided tour of the university library at the beginning of your course and it's important to use this opportunity to get a feel of what is available and how you can access it. It won't all sink in, but you'll have a rough map in your head of what you can use, and you can follow this up later with specific questions to a librarian. Librarians are extraordinarily nice and helpful nowadays and they have told me personally that they *want* students to ask questions. So, go ahead and ask. Imagine that they have one of those 'Ask me' notices pinned on their backs.

'The only thing that you absolutely have to know, is the location of the library.'
Albert Einstein

'The more that you read, the more things you will know. The more that you learn, the more places you'll go.'
Dr. Seuss

Searching in the library

When you've mastered the basic searches in your library system, it's a good time to find 'Advanced Search' on the search screen. This will give you more options and allow you to narrow down your search and make it more focused.

Tricks for taking aim

When you get a bit more familiar with the library search facilities, you'll want to be able to focus your searches more precisely. You can try using some of the following:

Cool Boolean tools

You can often use Boolean operators **'AND'**, **'OR'** and **'NOT'** to combine keywords.

Use OR to identify any source which mentions either of the words (or phrases). For example,

"antidepressants" OR "anxiolytics"

This will find articles that are about either antidepressants or anxiolytics (or, indeed, both together).

Keywords – single words (or very short phrases) that describe topic areas or subjects. Sometimes these are defined and limited according to a journal's or database's **thesaurus**.

Use AND to combine two (or more) different concepts. For example,

"antidepressants" AND "anxiolytics"

This will find articles which are about both antidepressants and anxiolytic drugs. You could add AND "effectiveness" so that it became "antidepressants" AND "anxiolytics" AND "effectiveness" which would only find articles that are about the effectiveness of these two classes of drugs.

Use NOT to exclude items from the search. For example, if you enter

"antidepressants" AND "anxiolytics" AND "effectiveness" NOT "USA"

The database will find articles that are about the effectiveness of these two classes of drugs, but exclude any that contain any reference to the USA.

Wildcards

When you're playing cards, a wildcard is a card that can have any value, suit or colour. It's the same in library searching, except instead of cards, we're talking about letters of the alphabet, and wildcards let you look for alternative spellings of an expression. There are different kinds of wildcard:

- First, there's '*', which tells the computer: 'Accept any number of any letters here and after this'. So, when I'm looking for an article on the topic of 'inclusion', there are many ways of expressing this: inclusion, inclusive, inclusivity, inclusiveness, and so on. Authors choose to express their ideas in different ways. So, I will rarely use the actual word 'inclusion' when searching, since article authors may not have thought to express their idea in terms of this actual word. So, I will use 'inclus*' since this contains the wildcard '*' which tells the database: 'Find all words that begin with "inclus" and which have any number of any letters coming after "inclus".

- The wildcard '?' is similar to '*' but subtly different, and more useful for alternative spellings. It's particularly useful where there is an alternative US/UK spelling. Friends in America spell 'organisation' as 'organization', so if I want to make sure I find all mentions of organisation or organization, I'll enter 'organi?ation'. So the '?' wildcard tells the database: 'accept ANY letter in this position, but ONLY this position'.

Quotation marks

Quotation marks let you search for specific phrases. For example, searching for 'proteolytic maturation of proprotein substrates' will only find occurrences of this exact phrase. (There can't be many.) Quotation marks will work this way in Google and Google Scholar as well.

Other search limiters

Most databases will let you to filter your search as follows:

- Publication date: You might only want sources from the last 10 years.

- Publication type: Are you looking for articles, websites, statistics, grey literature, or all of the above?

- Country of origin: You can restrict your search results by looking just for materials coming from one country. And remember that some databases draw far more heavily than others on US-based sources.

ACTIVITY # Test your knowledge with the activities below

1 How might you use a wildcard when you are looking for these words?

- Encyclopaedia / encyclopedia

- Exclusion

- Computer programs

2 Desperately seeking 'Confucian'

- Think how you might use Boolean operators and wildcards when searching for the topic 'Confucian'.

Remember, when finding an article or a book in the library ...

University libraries get access to packages of journals (for which they pay large amounts of money) and to which you will have free access via databases and portals, which we'll look at in Section 6. Be prepared to invest an hour or two playing with your library's website to see what's on offer.

There are other resources for hunting down books which may not be in your university library's stock:

- **WorldCat** is a catalogue of major libraries throughout the world which can show the location of specific titles in the libraries nearest to you.

- **The Library of Congress catalogue** is a major catalogue which is often used to check bibliographic details of hard-to-find books.

- **Bookdata Online** is a database of books in print available from UK and US publishers. It can search for chapters or sections within books as well as by title, author, and publisher, and it also keeps details of books which have gone out of print.

- **Amazon** is also a good resource for finding books (but not articles). It's not as good as Google Book Search but it does have some useful features such as 'Look Inside!' which allows you to look at the contents pages and to read selected pages, the index, and some other information.

> 'If you want to get laid, go to college. If you want an education, go to the library.'
>
> Frank Zappa

Inter-library loan

If the worst comes to the worst and you really can't get access to an unusual piece of literature or a key book, you can get it via inter-library loan, either electronically, or as a photocopy. Ask your librarian about this. There will probably be a charge, but it won't be nearly as much as it would be from a publisher's website.

Subject guides in the library

There should be an A-Z list of subject guides on your library website, and when you click on your subject of interest, the resulting page will offer all kinds of advice and pointers to resources, databases, and websites on your subject.

Check your knowledge with the questions below

	✓	Notes
1 Have you had a tour of the library, or asked a librarian for guidance?		
2 Have you used the library search box?		
3 Have you experimented with any of the library databases, using wildcards, or other ways of focusing your search?		

What's a database? And why is it good for me?

10 second summary

A database is just a big bag with lots of information in it – organized information that you can find easily.

Databases, portals, and platforms

- A database can be described as a big electronic bag with lots of organized and streamlined information in it. The information has been organized by **fields**: keywords, authors, titles, etc., and these fields of information can be searched.

- A portal, by contrast, is like a gateway through which you can find databases, books, links, and other sites: it's like a mega-database. You'll find both databases and portals under 'Databases' in your library website.

- A platform is the interface used by a database provider. From the platform you can access different databases, but they'll all have the same interface.

Don't worry too much about whether you're in a database, a portal, or a platform. The main thing to remember is that these facilities aren't search engines, like Google, and you'll need to specify more exactly what you want to find. The reward for the extra work will be in the richness of your findings.

A student told us

'I'm completely confused by all the databases.'

Yes, it's like a maze. Don't give up: go to a librarian if you're not finding what you want.

More on portals and platforms

These give you access to databases, books, journals, and other information and are a bit like libraries in themselves. Often, your library will direct you through these to find what you're looking for. Here are a few:

ProQuest

ProQuest is a platform which, according to its blurb, hosts collections spanning six centuries, all disciplines, and diverse content types. It's especially good for the lesser-known collections and for historical sources, such as old newspapers.

EBSCO

EBSCO is a platform giving you access to research databases, journals, magazines, and ePackages, e-books, and much more.

Tip

Try Kopernio. This lets you use your favourite tools (e.g. Web of Science, Google Scholar, PubMed, etc.) and gives you automatic access to a pdf of an article that you're interested in. It puts a 'button' in your browser toolbar, which then gives access to a 'locker' which holds the pdfs.

JSTOR

JSTOR provides access to more than 12 million academic journal articles, books, and primary sources in 75 disciplines.

DOAJ (Directory of Open Access Journals)

DOAJ – at https://doaj.org/ – provides access to high-quality, open access, peer-reviewed journals.

OVID

OVID is a platform which gives access to journals, books, collections, 100 core and niche databases, and other platforms. It ranges over a wide range of topics on medicine, healthcare, dentistry, and sports science.

Web of Science

The Web of Science isn't just about science, and is more than just a platform. It gives you 'leads' to all of the articles published on a particular subject, or by a particular author, in reputable peer-review journals over a certain timespan.

Tip

Take a look at the online tutorials on how to use Web of Science. To find them, type 'Web of Science quick tour' into your search engine and look for the YouTube guides.

NICE

NICE is the National Institute for Healthcare and Excellence (UK), and its Evidence portal www.evidence.nhs.uk/ gives access to a range of information relating to health.

Zetoc

Zetoc describes itself as 'one of the world's most comprehensive research databases, giving you access to over 34,500 journals and more than 55 million article citations and conference papers through the British Library's electronic table of contents'. Zetoc is particularly useful as it includes an email alert service to help you to keep up to date with relevant new articles and papers. You could, for example, tell it to send you all articles by a certain author.

> **Abstract** – a brief summary (usually 150–350 words) of a research project and its findings.

Scopus

Scopus is a huge abstract and citation database containing peer-reviewed research literature and quality web sources.

> **Citation** – a mention of, or quotation from, a book, paper, or author, using one of several systems of referencing (e.g. Harvard, APA).

Tip

Remember – always log in to these services via your library website, or you won't get beyond the first page or two. Your library has paid mega-bucks for them and you can only access them via your library's account.

Specific subject databases

Aside from the generic databases, there are also specific databases for particular subjects. There are many subject-specific databases; see below for some useful suggestions:

British Nursing Index

The clue's is in the name. It covers 200 journals and other English-language titles.

Business Source Premier

Covers management, economics, finance, accounting, international business, marketing.

Tip

Most university libraries offer resource lists in which you'll find direct access to all your own personal course readings and resources. They will enable you to access all the most important materials wherever you are – using whatever device is convenient: phone, tablet, laptop, or desktop.

ERIC

ERIC is paid for by the United States Department of Education, and provides access to over 1 million records on education, including the 'grey literature' of, for example, fact sheets.

Sociological abstracts

Abstracts and indexes the international literature of sociology and related disciplines in the social and behavioural sciences.

BEI

The BEI is the British Education Index, which is the British equivalent of ERIC.

Embase

A biomedical and pharmaceutical database indexing over 3,500 international journals in drug research, pharmacology, and related topics.

TIP

BrowZine is a great resource to help you find relevant journals and save articles from them. All the articles you save will stay in sync between all your devices, which you can then use wherever you are – on a plane, train, or in a car. Ask your librarian about it.

HMIC (Health Management Information Consortium)

Combines a number of databases, with abstracts of journal articles, monographs, reports, and government documents, all focusing on health policy and management.

PubMed

If you work in healthcare, including medicine, you will almost certainly want access to PubMed, which is the US repository for biomedical literature.

CINAHL

For students of nursing and allied health disciplines, CINAHL offers, as the producers put it, 'the definitive research tool for nursing and allied health professionals'.

PsycINFO

Primarily for psychologists, PsycINFO is run by the American Psychological Association and contains 4.2 million records in the behavioural sciences and mental health.

OpenGrey

This gives free access to nearly one million references of grey literature from Europe.

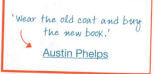

'Wear the old coat and buy the new book.'

Austin Phelps

Grey literature – writings not produced by commercial publishers. They include research reports, working papers, **conference** papers and **proceedings, theses, preprints,** and reports from government and business.

Preprint – a version of a scholarly paper that precedes formal publication in an academic journal. The preprint will have been accepted for publication but not fully copy edited or typeset, and in this form it usually appears in open-access form in an author's institutional repository.

References – all the books and articles referred to in a research report or article, appearing in a list in a standard format (such as the Harvard system) at the end of the report.

A student told us

'My keywords are not working in the database.'

Databases often have their own thesaurus of subject headings. You can sometimes use the thesaurus words alongside your keywords to help your filtering.

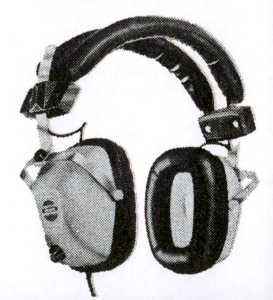

Got it

	✓	Notes
1 Have you taken a couple of hours to explore Web of Science?		
2 Have you tried ProQuest?		
3 Have you opened the database relating to your own subject interest?		

Where do I find stuff that's not in the big databases?

10 second summary

Hard-to-find sources such as statistics, theses, and images are available online, often in specialist databases.

60 second summary

There are many great places to find useful information online which are often neglected by students, but provide really insightful and detailed data for you to use. These include official statistics, data produced by charities, big organizations and governments, theses, and digital photographs and videos. These types of resources are often found via specialist databases or portals found on specific platforms.

Official statistics

These are the data produced by governments, NGOs (charities), and big organizations on various aspects of their work. For social scientists, geographers, and many others, they offer a remarkably useful resource. Yet they are used surprisingly little by students.

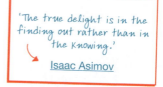

'The true delight is in the finding out rather than in the knowing.'

Isaac Asimov

If you can show that you have drawn relevantly from these statistics, your work will be viewed all the more favourably. There is a variety of websites from which you can easily download data of extraordinary detail and richness, and this can often be manipulated in your own spreadsheet remarkably simply.

Check out these useful links:

http://stats.oecd.org/wbos/ provides a wide range of statistics gathered by the Organisation for Economic Co-operation and Development (OECD). It covers everything from agriculture and fisheries, to social protection and well-being.

www.usa.gov/statistics gives data about the USA, such as maps and population, demographic, and economic data.

www.ons.gov.uk/ – the UK Office for National Statistics, the US equivalent, for the UK.

OFFSTATS is a New Zealand-based resource offering especially statistics on government, politics, and the media.

The Statistical Abstract of the United States is the digest of statistics coming from the US census and focuses on the social, political, and economic organization of the USA.

UNdata http://data.un.org/ is the United Nations collation of country data services, with particularly useful areas on crime and education. The latter includes links to a broad range of other databases including those of UNESCO and the OECD.

The World Factbook is produced by the CIA (yes, really, the CIA – the Central Intelligence Agency). As it describes itself, it 'provides information on the history, people, government, economy, geography, communications, transportation, military, and transnational issues for 267 world entities'. (I know what you're thinking … the CIA? But really, it's good.)

Gapminder http://www.gapminder.org/ gives fascinating interactive social statistics.

Theses

A thesis (plural: theses) is a write-up of an extended piece of scholarly work, usually from a doctorate. Theses can provide invaluable help on precisely targeted subjects, though you should remember not to use other people's theses as a model for your own, since they are of highly variable quality. The following platforms are great places to find useful theses:

Thesis (plural: **theses**) – an extended piece of original scholarly work based on research. Usually used to refer to the write-up of work based on doctoral research. A write-up of a shorter work, for example of a masters-based or undergraduate project, may be called a 'dissertation'.

ProQuest (see page 64) claims to host the world's largest collection of dissertations and theses from international sources.

EThOS is the British Library's digital repository of all doctoral theses completed at UK institutions. Theses can provide invaluable help on precisely targeted subjects. Remember, though, that theses are of highly variable quality.

To search further afield for relevant theses, you can try:

Networked Digital Library of Theses and Dissertations

DART-Europe e-Theses: open-access theses from Europe

Images and videos

Now that digital photographs and videos are free and disposable, image-based methods provide a powerful extension to data collection. Data may be collected in photographs, videos, films, graffiti, drawings, cartoons, and so on. For ideas on how to use images in social research, look at Photovoice, which is a participatory action research platform which aims to use photography to enable grassroots social action.

Images can easily be transferred via social networking services such as WhatsApp, Flickr, and Instagram.

Here are some good ways of finding images online:

Box of Broadcasts (BoB)

Box of Broadcasts (BoB) is an off-air recording and media archive service. It lets you record TV and radio programmes, and podcasts scheduled to broadcast over the next seven days, as well as retrieving programmes from the last seven days.

Google images

In the Google 'results' page, click on 'Images' at the top right.

Word

When in a Word document, click on 'Insert' and then on 'Online Pictures' and type the name of whatever it is you want a picture of.

A student
told us

'I can't reference the images I'm using.'

You can do a reverse image search:

- Google Images lets you search by image by selecting the camera icon in the search box. Upload an image or search by its URL.

- TinEye does much the same as Google Images.

Do the following tasks to make sure you get it

	✓	Notes
1 Try opening http://data.un.org/ and look for figures on International Migrants.		
2 Open Gapminder at http://www.gapminder.org/ and try the interactive tool showing the relationship between income and life expectancy.		
3 Find a thesis on your topic of interest.		

Who will help me?

10 second summary

Librarians will help you, obviously. And your tutors. But also try social networking with specialist websites that connect you with others doing academic work.

60 second summary

Finding support

Technology is continuously changing, and very rapidly. I've concentrated so far on the ways that you can, as a solitary researcher, use technology to find sources, but new technology lets you join with others in social networks. Once you have built a network of people with interests similar to yours, you can use them to identify new sources and resources. You can become a participant in a community – not just a consumer of information.

Get involved

You may be able to increase the range, diversity, and number of people who can get involved in your work. You'll be able to connect with them to get new ideas and plug in to their reading lists and resources, which may be completely different from your own.

You may find out new information on what key academics in your field of study are doing and thinking from sites such as Academia.edu. You can 'follow' key names and discover what they are currently publishing.

Or, on Twitter, follow relevant hashtags, which help to create a sense of community in the lonely process of doing research.

Useful platforms

Some of these social networking services are specifically for academic work – some, such as MethodSpace give you an entry to high-quality discussion. Others may be familiar, but you may not have considered using them for your academic work:

- **MethodSpace** (www.methodspace.com) is a social networking service for social scientists run by the publisher Sage. As well as networking, it offers video clips and advice.

- **ResearchGate** (www.researchgate.net) offers networking with other researchers (mostly professional researchers) and a search engine that browses academic databases.

- **Graduate Junction** (www.graduatejunction.net) is a social networking service aimed at postgraduates and postdoctoral researchers.

- **Academia.edu** enables you to connect with professional researchers and to keep updated with their latest publications.

- **Twitter** is useful for connecting with others who have similar interests via hashtags. Try ones such as #ResearchMethods, #phdchat, #PhDlife, #reading, #grantwriting or you can try a twitter address such as @ReliableSources (which is about politics in the newspapers).

- **WhatsApp messaging** lets you set up your own group for discussing new ideas, references, or images.

- **CiteULike** finds references, helps you manage them, and puts you in touch with other students.

- **YouTube** videos may help with certain subjects, though they are of very variable quality.

- **INVOLVE** gives guidance on the use of social media to actively involve people in research. Available at: http://www.invo.org.uk/wp-content/uploads/2014/11/9982-Social-Media-Guide-WEB.pdf (retrieved 19 February 2019).

- **Blogs** – reflections, commentaries, etc. kept online by some academics and researchers in which they may give details of current work. You can sometimes get access to these via Twitter, or look on key academics' university webpages.

With others, you can call out for help, moan, commiserate, and (hopefully) celebrate when you find an excellent source.

A student told us

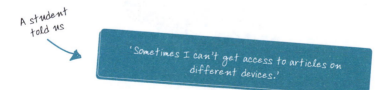

'Sometimes I can't get access to articles on different devices.'

Make sure that you log in to your library account, or you won't be able to access the full range of download facilities.

Risks

There are particular risks in opening yourself up on social media, so be savvy:

- Develop social media identities separate from your personal ones. Participants can then befriend you in a professional rather than a personal context.

- Always give an accurate portrayal of yourself on social media websites, but don't give away too many personal details.

- Ensure that you don't spread friends' personal information in ways that could identify them.

- Consider listing a privacy policy on any webpages you develop.

Filter for quality

You can get bogged down in social media, being bombarded (if you're not careful) with a lot of junk as well as the occasional jewel. So it's important to filter with the mnemonic **DIPER** – standing for Discard, Ignore, Park, Engage, Read (Adapted from: Research Information Network (2011) *Social Media: A Guide for Researchers*). With each tweet (or whatever) do a DIPER check (if only in your head):

Delete – have a quick read, and delete if it's obviously no use

Ignore – if it's slanderous, abusive, or otherwise empty; then delete

Park – if looks like it may be worth considering; worth coming back to

Engage – if you think it may be interesting – read and assess

Read – engage fully and reply if appropriate

'Smart phones and social media expand our universe. We can connect with others or collect information easier and faster than ever.'

Daniel Goleman

Got it?

	✓	Notes
Have you logged on with any of the social networking services mentioned in this section?		

Why can't I find anything?

10 second summary

If you can't find anything you'll need to broaden your field of vision. To open up your vista, you can draw a mind-map, try 'snowballing', or there are various tricks you can use with data-bases to focus your search.

60 second
summary

Still can't find anything?

You can't find anything on your topic of interest? It may be the case that you are not using enough search facilities, or, more likely, that you are making your search too narrow. You are pinpointing your search terms too finely, or throwing away related information that is not on the precise subject of your interest, but is connected, and therefore useful. Remember that any literature review you do ultimately will not be on the exact topic of your research, but rather it will be on the more general subject surrounding your research.

'I keep coming up with the same sources.'

If you enter any search term into Google Scholar, it will offer you alternative search terms in 'Related searches', and these can be really useful for thinking laterally and broadening your ideas.

If you are still struggling, have a go at this exercise:

ACTIVITY Draw a mindmap

If you were a psychology student and wanted to look at *austerity and how it affects the incidence of depression* and you are coming up with nothing useful, it may be that you are searching too specifically. Your searches may need to go broader. So, think about the broader ways that your question may be framed. Think about alternative search terms, such as *mental health, recession, financial crisis, inequality*. If you draw a mindmap or a storyboard in which you connect these ideas, as below, you may even come up with new ideas.

Here's what one may look like:

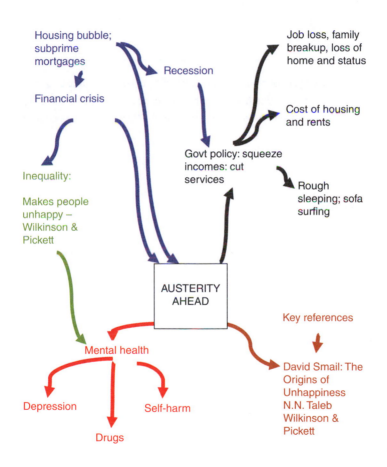

Snowballing

Snowballing is probably the best searching strategy that I personally use. Revisit Section 4 for details.

Fan out

Fan out from your original topic or question by dividing it into topics, and then think of keywords that might be associated with those topics. Try brainstorming this with other students. See the 'fanning out' DIY activity below.

 **ACTIVITY** Fanning out

Use this diagram to help you 'fan out' from your original question to think of topics within it and keywords that derive from the topics:

'Judge people by their questions rather than their answers.'

Voltaire

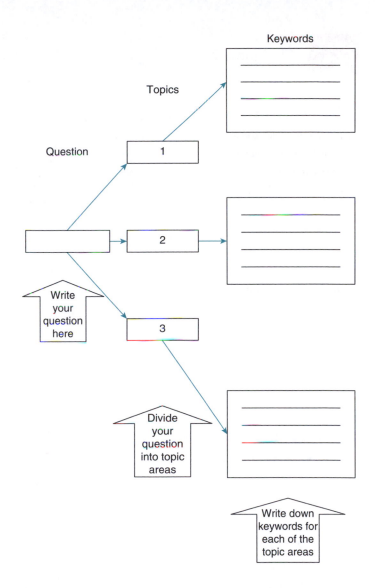

CHECK POINT Tried these?

	✓	Notes
1 Have you tried dividing your research question into topics and keywords?		
2 Have you used 'snowballing'?		
3 Have you drawn a mindmap of a particular research area or question?		

Final checklist: How to know you are done

To make sure you have mastered all you need to know, work through this final checklist.

	✓	Notes
1 Do you have a clear idea of the sources likely to be important in your subject?		
2 Do you have a good idea of the quality of sources? What makes a good source?		
3 What characterizes a primary source?		
4 Have you explored all the features of Google Scholar?		

	✓	Notes
5 Have you had a tour of the library and found your key subject database and played around with it?		
6 Have you looked at any of the general databases (or 'portals') that give you access to many other databases?		
7 Have you tried connecting with others on social media?		
8 Have you tried mindmapping or snowballing to open up your search?		

Glossary

Abstract a brief summary (usually 150–350 words) of a research project and its findings.

Article a write-up of research or scholarship in a **journal**, presenting research findings or discussing topics of interest.

Bibliography a list of books and articles of interest. Not to be confused with **references**, which are all of the books and articles referred to in a research report or article (and no more).

Citation a mention of, or quotation from, a book, paper, or author, using one of several systems of referencing (e.g. Harvard, APA).

Conference a gathering of academics, professionals, and students meeting to discuss topics in a subject area.

Grey literature writings not produced by commercial publishers. They include research reports, working papers, **conference** papers and **proceedings**, **theses**, **preprints**, and reports from government and business.

Journal   a periodical which carries **articles** (usually **peer-review**ed) on topics of interest (usually arising from research) to academics and students of a subject.

Keywords   single words (or very short phrases) that describe topic areas or subjects. Sometimes these are defined and limited according to a journal's or database's **thesaurus**.

Literature review   an organized review of books, articles, and published research on a specific topic to discover themes, gaps, inconsistencies, agreements.

Paper   an **article**, but 'paper' usually refers to a presentation (which may be written up later for **proceedings**) given at a **conference** or **symposium**.

Peer-review   a system used by editors of scholarly journals to assess the quality of work submitted for publication. Submissions to a peer-review journal will be assessed by two or more experts in a field, and using these assessments a journal editor will judge whether a submission is worthy of publication. Publication in a peer-review journal is taken to be the most robust assurance of an article's quality.

Preprint   a version of a scholarly paper that precedes formal publication in an academic journal. The preprint will have been accepted for publication but not fully copy edited or typeset, and in this form it usually appears in open-access form in an author's institutional repository.

Primary source   a direct account of what has been done or observed. Compare with **secondary source.**

Proceedings   papers that have been presented at a **conference** or **symposium** and have been been printed in a collection of 'proceedings'.

References   all the books and articles referred to in a research report or article, appearing in a list in a standard format (such as the Harvard system) at the end of the report.

Secondary source   is a presentation of, and/or reworking of, usually, many **primary sources**.

Sources   sources of evidence such as literature, personal experience, testimony, documents, archives, artefacts. In academic life (and in this book), we are mainly talking about literature of one kind or another.

Symposium   like a **conference**, but on a more specific topic within the subject area. Papers given at symposia are often published in **proceedings**.

Thesis (plural: **theses**)   an extended piece of original scholarly work based on research. Usually used to refer to the write-up of work based on doctoral research. A write-up of a shorter work, for example of a masters-based or undergraduate project, may be called a 'dissertation'.

Further reading and resources

EasyBib at http://www.easybib.com/guides/students/writing-guide/ii-research/a-finding-sources/

Provides simple access to an array of databases, books, and articles as well as advice on using sources.

Fink, A. (2005) *Conducting Research Literature Reviews: From the Internet to Paper*. London: Sage.

Systematic, with good examples on searching in health, education, and business domains. Not just the process, but also good on evaluating the articles you select.

Shon, P. (2019) *Cite Your Source.* London: Sage.